NATIONAL GEOGRAPHIC

Best Friends

Marvin Buckley

My family plays games.

My family plays music.

My family goes riding.

My family goes to concerts.

My family likes dogs.

My family likes cats.

Our families are different
but we are best friends.